Isaac H Albright

Revival hymns and choruses

Isaac H Albright

Revival hymns and choruses

ISBN/EAN: 9783337335397

Printed in Europe, USA, Canada, Australia, Japan

Cover: Foto ©Lupo / pixelio.de

More available books at **www.hansebooks.com**

"I will sing with the spirit, and I will sing with the understanding also." *I Cor. 14-15.*

REVIVAL HYMNS

AND

CHORUSES,

COMPILED BY

REV. ISAAC H. ALBRIGHT

FOURTH EDITION.

PRICE 10 CENTS PER COPY. $1.00 PER DOZEN.

Copyright 1891 by D. W. Crider.

YORK, PA.:
PUBLISHED BY CRIDER & BRO.
1891.

PREFACE.

The compiler of this work has long felt the need of a small collection of hymns and choruses, suitable for use in seasons of religious interest; so cheap that all can buy them; so familiar that all can sing them. These hymns and choruses have been gathered from many sources. When we knew that a hymn was copy-right property, and its author was known, we secured permission to use it in our little book. We are under great obligations to our friends who have granted us this permission. With the desire that God's blessing may greatly attend its use, the work is sent forth on its mission of service.

THE COMPILER.

REVIVAL HYMNS AND CHORUSES.

— 1 —

Christ Knocking at the Door.

1 Behold a stranger at the door!
He gently knocks, has knocked before,
Has waited long—is waiting still:
You treat no other friend so ill.

Cho: O, let the dear Savior come in,
He'll cleanse thy heart from sin!
O, keep Him no more, out at the door,
But let the dear Savior come in.

2 O lovely attitude, He stands
With melting heart and bleeding hands,
O matchless kindness, and He shows
This matchless kindness to His foes!

3 But will He prove a friend indeed?
He will; the very friend you need;
The Friend of sinners—yes, 'tis He
With garments dyed on Calvary.

4 Rise, touched with gratitude divine;
Turn out His enemy and thine,
That soul destroying monster, sin,
And let the heavenly Stranger in.

5 Admit Him ere His anger burn;
His feet departed ne'er return;
Admit Him, or the hour's at hand,
You'll at His door rejected stand.

— 2 —
Sinners Entreated.

1 Come, ye sinners, poor and needy,
  Weak and wounded, sick and sore;
Jesus ready stands to save you,
  Full of pity, love and power:
    He is able,
  He is willing, doubt no more.

2 Now ye needy, come and welcome,
  God's free bounty glorify;
True belief and true repentance,
  Every grace that brings you nigh;
    Without money,
  Come to Jesus Christ and buy.

3 Let not conscience make you linger
  Nor of fitness fondly dream;
All the fitness He requireth
  Is to feel your need of Him:
    This He gives you;
  'Tis the Spirit's glim'ring beam.

CHORUSES.

— 1 —

Turn to the Lord, and seek salvation,
  Sound the praise of His dear name;
Glory, honor and salvation,
  Christ the Lord is come again.

— 2 —

O believe him ; O receive him—
  There is none like Christ, my God :
He is near thee ; He will cheer thee—
  Only trust in Jesus' blood.

— 3 —

Doubting sinner,
  Doubt not, but believe,
He who saved ten thousand others
  He will thee receive.

— 3 —

And Yet There is Room.

1 Come, sinners, to the gospel feast,
  Let every soul be Jesus' guest ;
  Ye need not one be left behind,
  For God hath bidden all mankind.

2 Sent by my Lord, on you I call,
  The invitation is to all ;
  Come all the world ! come sinner thou !
  All things in Christ are ready now.

3 Come all ye souls by sin oppress'd,
  Ye restless wanderers after rest ;
  Ye poor and maim'd, and halt and blind,
  In Christ a hearty welcome find.

4 My message as from God receive,
  Ye all may come to Christ and live,
  O let His love your heart constrain,
  Nor suffer Him to die in vain.

5 This is the time, no more delay,
The invitation is to-day;
Come in this moment at His call,
And live for Him who died for all.

CHORUSES.

— 1 —

O come and will you go,
  Will you go, will you go,
O come will you go,
  Where pleasures never die.

— 2 —

Come along, come along,
  Come all the way along;
Come along, come along,
  And love the dying Lamb.

— 3 —

Come along, come along,
  Obey the word of God,
For why will you die in your sins.

— 4 —

Come home, come home,
O prodigal child, come home,
Come home, come home,
O prodigal child, come home.

— 4 —

Down at the Cross.

1 Down at the cross where my Savior died,
Down, where for cleansing from sin I cried;
There to my heart was the blood applied;
  Glory to his name.

CHORUS.—Glory to his name,
Glory to his name,
There to my heart was the blood applied,
Glory to his name.

2 I am so wondrously saved from sin,
Jesus so sweetly abides within;
There at the cross where He took me in,
Glory to his name.

3 O, precious fountain, that saves from sin,
I am so glad I have entered in;
There Jesus saves me and keeps me clean,
Glory to his name.

4 Come to this fountain, so rich and sweet;
Cast thy poor soul at the Savior's feet;
Plunge in to-day, and be made complete;
Glory to his hame.

— 5 —
Almost Persuaded.

1 "Almost persuaded," now to believe;
"Almost persuaded," Christ to receive;
Seems now some soul to say,
"Go, Spirit, go Thy way.
Some more convenient day
On Thee I'll call."

2 "Almost persuaded," come, come to-day;
"Almost persuaded," turn not away;
Jesus invites you here,
Angels are ling'ring near,
Prayers rise from hearts so dear :
O wanderer, come.

3 "Almost persuaded," harvest is past!
"Almost persuaded," doom comes at last!
"Almost" can not avail;
"Almost" is but to fail!
Sad, sad, that bitter wail—
"Almost—*but lost!*"

— 6 —
Come to Jesus.

Come to Jesus, come to Jesus,
Come to Jesus just now,
Just now come to Jesus,
Come to Jesus just now.

He will save you.
Oh, believe Him.
He is able.
He is willing.
He'll receive you.
Flee to Jesus.
Look unto Him.
Only trust Him.
Call upon Him.

He will hear you.
He'll have mercy.
He'll forgive you.
He will cleanse you.
He'll renew you.
He will clothe you.
Jesus loves you.
Don't reject Him.
Hallelujah. Amen.

— 7 —
Don't Wait for To-Morrow.

1 O, come to the Savior to-day,
'Tis folly to wait till to-morrow;
Then will you longer delay?
To-morrow may fill you with sorrow.

Cho.—The Savior is calling to-day,
O, bring him your trouble and sorrow,
Come, bow at his footstool and pray,
It may be too late on to-morrow.

2 O, look at the cross where he died,
　　And think of his anguish and sorrow,
　Then give up your folly and pride,
　　It may be too late on to-morrow.

3 How many have gone to the grave,
　　Whose end was destruction and horror,
　O, would you have Jesus to save :
　　Then wait not to seek him to-morrow.

4 Then fly to the Savior to-day,
　　And walk in the way that is narrow,
　'Twill lead you from folly away,
　　And give you a joyous to-morrow.

— 8 —

Come to the Fountain.

1 O come to-day to the fountain,
　　That flows for you and for me ;
　O, come, and drink of its waters,
　　They flow ever full and free.

Cho.—Come to the clear flowing fountain,
　　　Flowing for you and for me :
　　Drink of the life-giving fountain,
　　　Its waters are pure and free.

2 O sinner burdened with sorrow,
　　How sweet the message to thee :
　O, come to-day to the fountain,
　　That flows ever full and free.

3 O sinner, look unto Jesus,
　　Who conquered death and the grave ;
　He bids you come to the fountain,
　　Its waters have power to save.

4 Why will you wander in darkness?
   Why to the world will you cling?
O, come and plunge in the fountain,
   And you shall be free from sin.

— 9 —

Sorrow for the Suffering of the Savior.

1 Alas! and did my Savior bleed,
   And did my Sov'reign die?
Would He devote that sacred head
   For such a worm as I?

2 Was it for crimes that I have done
   He groan'd upon the tree?
Amazing pity! grace unknown!
   And love beyond degree.

3 Well might the sun in darkness hide,
   And shut his glories in,
When Christ the mighty Maker died
   For man the creature's sin.

4 Thus might I hide my blushing face,
   While his dear cross appears;
Dissolve my heart in thankfulness,
   And melt mine eyes to tears.

5 But drops of grief can ne'er repay
   The debt of love I owe;
Here, Lord, I give myself away,
   'Tis all that I can do.

CHORUSES.

— 1 —

O look away, O look away,
  O look away to Calvary :
To Calvary, to Calvary,
  O look away to Calvary.

— 2 —

He loves me, he loves me,
  He loves me, this I know,
He gave himself to die for me,
  Because he loves me so.

— 3 —

Jesus is good to me,
Jesus is good to me,
So good, so good,
Jesus is good to my soul.

— 4 —

Help me, dear Savior, thee to own,
  And ever faithful be ;
And when thou sittest on thy throne,
  Dear Lord, remember me.

— 5 —

Jesus died for you,
  Jesus died for me,
Yes, Jesus died for all mankind,
  Bless God, salvation's free.

— 6 —

I'll never forget thee,
  I'll never forget thee, Lord,
I'll never forget thee,
  Dear Lord remember me

I can, and I will, and I do believe,
　I can, and I will, and I do believe,
I can, and I will, and I do believe,
　That Jesus died for me.

— 8 —

Look away, look away,
　Look away to Calvary,
Look away, look away,
　Look away to Calvary.

— 9 —

Dear Jesus receive me,
　No more will I grieve thee,
O blessed Redeemer,
　O save me at the cross.

— 10 —

O! 'twas love, 'twas wondrous love!
　The love of God to me:
It brought my Savior from above,
　To die on Calvary.

— 11 —

Only believe, and you shall be saved,
　Only believe and you shall be saved,
Only believe, and you shall be saved,
　And heaven is yours forever.

— 12 —

The half was never told,
　The half was never told,
Of grace divine, so wonderful,
　The half was never told.

— 13 —

O, how I love Jesus,
 O, how I love Jesus,
O, how I love Jesus,
 Because he first loved me.

— 14 —

He loves me, this I know,
 He loves me this I know,
I know, I feel it's true,
 He loves me, this I know.

— 15 —

Come to Jesus, come to Jesus,
 Come to Jesus now,
He will save you, he will save you,
 He will save you now.

— 16 —

O, you must be a lover of the Lord,
O, you must be a lover of the Lord,
O, you must be a lover of the Lord,
Or you can't go to heaven when you die.

— 17 —

Come to the fount of cleansing blood,
 That flows from Calvary ;
Thou shalt be made a child of God,
 And be forever free.

— 18 —

Jesus can save, and Jesus alone,
 Jesus alone, Jesus alone,
Jesus, my Lord and my Savior, I own,
 Jesus, my Savior I own.

— 19 —

I am sinking out of self, out of self into Christ,
  Sinking out of self into Christ,
Sinking, sinking, sinking out of self,
  Sinking out of self into Christ.

— 20 —

O, for converting grace,
  And O, for sanctifying power,
Lord we beg for Jesus sake
  A sweet refreshing shower.

— 21 —

Remember me, remember me,
  Dear Lord remember me!
Remember first thy dying groans,
  And then remember me.

— 22 —

Thy name blessed Jesus is all my plea;
  Dearest and sweetest name to me;
Thou art my shield and hiding place,
  I am redeemed by thy rich grace.

— 23 —

O, the Lamb, the loving Lamb,
  The Lamb of Calvary,
The Lamb that was slain, but liveth again,
  To intercede for me.

— 24 —

Only trust him, only trust him,
  Only trust him now;
He will save you, he will save you,
  He will save you now.

At the cross, at the cross, where I first saw the light,
And the burden of my heart rolled away,
It was there by faith I received my sight,
And now I am happy all the day.

— 26 —
Blessed be the name, blessed be the name,
Blessed be the name of the Lord.
Blessed be the name, blessed be the name,
Blessed be the name of the Lord.

— 10 —
Sufficiency of the Atonement.

1 There is a fountain filled with blood
Drawn from Immanuel's veins;
And sinners plunged beneath that flood,
Lose all their guilty stains.

2 The dying thief rejoiced to see
That fountain in his day;
O may I there, though vile as he,
Wash all my sins away.

3 Thou dying Lamb, Thy precious blood
Shall never lose its power,
Till all the ransomed church of God
Are saved to sin no more.

4 E'er since by faith, I saw the stream
Thy flowing wounds supply,
Redeeming love has been my theme,
And shall be till I die.

5 And when this feeble, faltering tongue
    Lies silent in the grave,
Then in a nobler, sweeter song,
    I'll sing thy power to save.

CHORUSES.

— 1 —

Worthy, worthy is the Lamb of God,
    Worthy, worthy is the Lamb of God,
Worthy, worthy is the Lamb of God,
    That taketh away the sin of the world.

— 2 —

O, the blood, the precious blood,
    That Jesus shed for me;
Upon the cross in crimson flood,
    Just now by faith I see.

— 3 —

O, redeemed, redeemed,
    Washed in the blood of the Lamb,
O redeemed, redeemed,
    Washed in the blood of the Lamb.

— 4 —

I do believe, I now believe,
    That Jesus died for me,
And thro' his blood, his precious blood
    I shall from sin be free.

— 5 —

The blood of Jesus cleanseth me,
    Cleanseth me, cleanseth me,
The blood of Jesus cleanseth me,
    As soon as I believe.

— 6 —

The cleansing stream, I see, I see!
I plunge, and Oh, it cleanseth me,
Oh, praise the Lord, it cleanseth me,
It cleanseth me, yes cleanseth me.

— 7 —

There's a fountain, a fountain, a fountain of love
  Ever flowing for you and for me,
This fountain cleanseth from all sin,
  And every sinner may now plunge in,
There's a fountain, a fountain, a fountain of love,
  Ever flowing for you and for me.

— 8 —

Jesus died for you,
  Jesus died for me,
Yes, Jesus died for all mankind,
  Bless God, salvation's free.

— 9 —

O precious blood, O cleansing blood,
  Drawn from Immanuel's veins,
And sinners plunge beneath that flood,
  Lose all their guilty stains.

— 10 —

My soul's been redeemed through the blood of the Lamb,
My soul's been redeemed through the blood of the Lamb,
  Been redeemed, been redeemed,
Been redeemed by the blood of the Lamb.

Why will you doubt him, when for you he died,
See, see the fountain is flowing from his side,
The poorest may partake of it and without money buy,
The Gospel call is free for all, and why should any die?

— 12 —

There is power in Jesus' blood,
  The is power in Jesus' blood,
There is power in Jesus' blood,
  To wash me white as snow.

Are you washed in the blood,
In the soul cleansing blood of the Lamb?
Are your garments spotless, are they white as snow?
Are you washed in the blood of the Lamb?

— 14 —

Savior wash me in the blood,
Savior wash me in the blood,
O wash me in the blood,
And I shall be whiter than the snow.

— 15 —

No other one but Jesus,
  No other one, no other one,
No other one but Jesus
  Can full salvation bring.

— 16 —

O, glorious fountain!
  Here will I stay,
And in thee ever
  Wash my sins away.

O who's like Jesus, O hallelujah,
  Praise ye the Lord ;
There's none like Jesus, O hallelujah,
  Love and serve the Lord.

— 18 —

    O, the bleeding lamb !
    O, the bleeding lamb !
    O, the bleeding lamb !
    Was found worthy.

— 11 —

What Hast Thou Done for Me?

1 I gave My life for thee,
   My precious blood I shed.
 That thou might'st randsomed be,
   And quickened from the dead;
 I gave, I gave My life for thee,
 What hast thou given for me?

2 My Father's house of light,—
   My glory-circled throne
 I left for earthly night,
   For wand'rings sad and lone ;
 I left, I left it all for thee,
 Hast thou left aught for Me?

3 I suffered much for thee,
   More than thy tongue could tell,
 Of bitterest agony,
   To rescue thee from hell;
 I've borne, I've borne it all for thee,
 What hast thou borne for me !

4 And I have brought to thee,
　　Down from My home above,
　Salvation full and free,
　　My pardon and My love;
　I bring, I bring rich gifts to thee,
　What hast thou brought to me?

— 12 —

The Judgment Day.

1 The judgment day is coming, coming, coming,
　The judgment day is coming,
　　On that great day!

Cho.—Let us take the wings of the morning,
　　　And fly away to Jesus;
　　Let us take the wings of the morning,
　　　And sound the jubilee.

2 You'll hear the trumpet sounding, sounding,
　　　sounding,
　You'll hear the trumpet sounding,
　　On that great day.

3 You'll see the Judge descending, descending,
　　　descending,
　You'll see the Judge descending,
　　On that great day.

4 You'll see the dead arising, arising, arising,
　You'll see the dead arising,
　　On that great day.

5 You'll hear the wicked wailing, wailing, wailing,
You'll hear the wicked wailing,
  On that great day.

CHO.—For they took not the wings of the morning,
   Nor flew away to Jesus;
  For they took not the wings of the morning,
   Nor sang the jubilee.

— 13 —
Diligence and Watchfulness.

1 A charge to keep I have,
  A God to glorify;
 A never-dying soul to save,
  And fit it for the sky.

2 To serve the present age,
  My calling to fulfill;
 O, may it all my powers engage,
  To do my Maker's will.

3 Arm me with jealous care,
  As in Thy sight to live,
 And O Thy servant, Lord, prepare,
  A strict account to give.

4 Help me to watch and pray,
  And on Thyself rely;
 Assured if I my trust betray,
  I shall forever die.

— 14 —
Lamb of God.

1 Not all the blood of beasts,
  On Jewish altars slain,

    Could give the guilty conscience peace,
       Or wash away the stain.

2 But Christ, the heav'nly Lamb
    Takes all our sins away;
 A sacrifice of nobler name,
    And richer blood than they.

3 My faith would lay her hand
    On that dear head of thine—
 While as a penitent I stand,
    And there confess my sin.

4 My soul looks back to see
    The burden thou didst bear,
 When hanging on the cursed tree,
    And hopes her guilt was there.

5 Believing, we rejoice
    To see the curse remove;
 We bless the Lamb with cheerful voice,
    And sing His bleeding love.

CHORUSES.

—1—

Jesus paid it all,
    All to Him I owe;
Sin had left a crimson stain,
He washed it white as snow.

—2—

I'll never turn back any more,
I'll never turn back any more,
For Jesus is there, he's gone to prepare,
    A home for you and for me.

— 3 —

I know that he'll answer my prayer,
I know that he'll answer my prayer,
  His promise is sure and I am secure,
I know that he'll answer my prayer.

— 4 —

We'll kneel around the altar,
We'll kneel around the altar,
We'll kneel around the altar,
  Where God will answer prayer.

— 5 —

There'll be no more sorrow there,
There'll be no more sorrow there,
  In heaven above where all is love,
There'll be no more sorrow there.

— 6 —

I am coming, Lord!
  Coming now to Thee!
Wash me, cleanse me, in the blood
  That flowed on Calvary.

— 7 —

I'm glad salvation's free!
I'm glad salvation's free;
Salvation's free for you and me,
I'm glad salvation's free!

— 8 —

We'll drive this battle on,
We'll drive this battle on,
In Jesus' might, we'll stand and fight,
And drive this battle on.

My Lord, deliverer of Daniel,
My Lord, deliverer of Daniel,
My Lord, deliverer of Daniel,
My Lord, deliver thou me.

— 15 —

Heavenly Joy on Earth.

1 Come we that love the Lord,
　And let your joys be known;
Join in a song with sweet accord,
　And thus surround the throne.

Cho.—We're marching to Zion,
　　Beautiful, beautiful Zion,
　We're marching upward to Zion,
　　That beautiful city of God.

2 The sorrows of the mind
　Be banished from the place;
Religion never was designed
　To make our pleasures less.

3 Let those refuse to sing
　Who never knew their God;
But children of the heav'nly King
　May speak their joys abroad.

4 The hill of Zion yields
　A thousand sacred sweets,
Before we reach the heavenly fields,
　Or walk the golden streets.

5 Then let our songs abound,
　And every tear be dry;

We're marching thro' Immanuel's ground,
To fairer worlds on high.

— 16 —
Rest for the Weary.

1 In the Christian's home in glory
There remains a land of rest;
There my Savior's gone before me
To fulfill my soul's request.

Cho.—There is rest for the weary,
There is rest for the weary,
There is rest for the weary,
There is rest for you;
On the other side of Jordan,
In the sweet fields of Eden,
Where the tree of life is blooming,
There is rest for you.

2 He is fitting up a mansion,
Which eternally shall stand;
For my stay shall not be transient,
In the holy, happy land.

3 Pain nor sickness ne'er shall enter,
Grief nor woe my lot shall share;
But in that celestial center,
I a crown of life shall wear.

— 17 —
Nothing but the Blood of Jesus.

1 What can wash away my stain?
Nothing but the blood of Jesus;
What can make me whole again?
Nothing but the blood of Jesus.

Cho.—Oh, precious is the flow
    That makes me white as snow;
    No other fount I know,
    Nothing but the blood of Jesus.

2 For my cleansing this I see—
    Nothing but the blood of Jesus;
  For my pardon this my plea—
    Nothing but the blood of Jesus.

3 Nothing can for sin atone—
    Nothing but the blood of Jesus,
  Naught of good that I have done—
    Nothing but the blood of Jesus.

4 This is all my hope and peace—
    Nothing but the blood of Jesus;
  This is all my righteousness—
    Nothing but the blood of Jesus.

5 Now by this I'll overcome—
    Nothing but the blood of Jesus;
  Now by this I'll reach my home—
    Nothing but the blood of Jesus.

6 Glory! glory! thus I sing—
    Nothing but the blood of Jesus;
  All my praise for this I bring—
    Nothing but the blood of Jesus.

— 18 —

The Judgment Day.

1 And must I be to judgment brought,
    And answer in that day,
  For every vain and idle thought,
    And every word I say?

2 Yes, every secret of my heart
    Shall shortly be made known,
And I receive my just desert
    For all that I have done.

3 How careful then ought I to live!
    With what religious fear,
Who such a strict account must give
    For my behavior here!

4 If now thou standest at the door,
    O let me feel thee near!
And make my peace with God, before
    I at thy bar appear.

CHORUSES.

— 1 —

We are passing away,
We are passing away,
We are passing away,
To the great Judgment day.

— 2 —

We're marching to the grave,
  We're marching to the grave, my friends,
We're marching to the grave,
  To lay this body down.

— 3 —

We are passing away,
We are passing away,
We'll soon, we'll soon be gone,

— 4 —

Fare you well, fare you well my old companions,
   Fare you well ;
I will no longer go with you
   The way to hell.

— 5 —

Weep, weep, mourn, mourn,
   Forsake your evil way ;
And to a smiling God return
   Before the Judgment day.

— 19 —

Memorial Hymn.

1 Come thou fount of every blessing,
   Tune my heart to sing thy grace ;
Streams of mercy, never ceasing ;
   Call for songs of loudest praise.

2 Teach me some melodious sonnet,
   Sung by flaming tongues above ;
Praise the mount—I'm fixed upon it,
   Mount of thy redeeming love.

3 Here I'll raise mine Ebenezer,
   Hither by thy help I'm come ;
And I hope by thy good pleasure,
   Safely to arrive at home.

4 Jesus sought me when a stranger,
   Wandering from the fold of God,
He, to rescue me from danger,
   Interposed his precious blood.

5 O! to grace how great a debtor,
　　Daily I'm constrained to be!
　Let thy goodness like a fetter,
　　Bind my wand'ring heart to thee.

6 Prone to wonder, Lord, I feel it;
　　Prone to leave the God I love—
　Here's my heart, oh, take and seal it;
　　Seal it for thy courts above.

CHORUSES.

— 1 —

My soul is reconciled,
　Glory, hallelujah;
My soul is reconciled,
　Praise ye the Lord.

— 2 —

I will sprinkle you with water,
　I will cleanse you from all sin;
Sanctify and make you holy,
　I will come and dwell within.

— 3 —

The fountain lies open,
The fountain lies open,
Come and bathe your weary soul.

— 4 —

O, how precious, O, how precious,
　Is the sound of Jesus' name;
O, how precious, O, how precious,
　Is the sound of Jesus' name.

— 5 —

I love Jesus, hallelujah,
    I love Jesus, yes, I do,
I do love Jesus, he's my Savior,
    Jesus smiles and loves me too.

— 6 —

Precious Jesus how I love thee,
    Upon this rock I stand,
I'm a poor mourning pilgrim,
    Bound for Canaan's happy land.

— 7 —

Hallelujah, hallelujah,
    We are on our journey home,
Hallelujah, hallelujah,
    We are on our journey home,

— 8 —

In my Father's house are many mansions,
    If it were not so I would have told you,
In my Father's house are many mansions,
    And all its streets are paved with gold.

— 9 —

Won't you come to Jesus?
Won't you come to Jesus?
Won't you come to Jesus?
    And be saved.

— 10 —

Blessed are the poor in spirit,
    Children of the Holy One,
They shall wear a crown of glory,
    When their work on earth is done.

— 11 —

Lord revive us, Lord revive us,
  All our help must come from thee,
Lord revive us, Lord revive us,
  All our help must come from thee.

— 12 —

I will arise and go to Jesus,
  He will embrace me in his arms,
In the arms of my dear Savior,
  O, there are ten thousand charms.

— 13 —

Precious Jesus ! come and make me whole
Holy Spirit, sanctify my soul.

— 14 —

Yes we'll gather at the river,
The beautiful, the beautiful river,
Gather with the saints at the river,
  In the beautiful city of God.

— 15 —

Close to Thee, close to Thee,
Close to Thee, close to Thee ;
All along my pilgrim journey,
Saviour draw me close to Thee.

— 16 —

We shall sleep, but not forever,
  There will be a glorious dawn,
We shall meet to part no never,
  On the resurrection morn.

— 17 —
Glory, glory be to Jesus,
   I am counting all but dross :
I have found a full salvation,
   I am resting at the cross,
I'm resting, I'm resting, I'm resting at the cross.

— 18 —
Hallelujah !
We shall love and praise forever,
Hallelujah !
Love and praise the Lord.

— 19 —
All I have I leave for Jesus,
   I am counting all but dross,
I am coming to the Master,
   I am clinging to the cross,
Clinging, clinging, clinging to the cross.

— 20 —
Fill me now, fill me now,
Jesus come and fill me now ;
Fill me with Thy hallow'd presence,
Come, oh, come and fill me now.

— 21 —
Cast your care on Jesus,
Cast your care on Jesus,
Cast your care on Jesus,
He will your burden bear.

— 22 —
We shall walk through the streets of the City,
   With the friends who have gone before,
We shall sit on the banks of the river,
   We shall meet to part no more.

— 23 —
O, angels guide me home,
Angels guide me home,
Angels guide me home,
  I long to be there.

— 24 —
Glory to the Father and the Son!
Glory to the Spirit, three in one!
Let us praise him, let us praise him,
Let us praise him to-day,
And sing his loving kindness on our way.

— 25 —
Glory, glory, hallelujah,
I rejoice salvation came;
Glory, glory, hallelujah,
I am saved in Jesus' name.

— 26 —
Hallelujah, hallelujah,
We are on our journey home;
Hallelujah, hallelujah,
We are on our journey home.

— 27 —
Won't you come to Jesus?
Won't you come to Jesus?
Won't you come to Jesus?
  And be saved.

— 28 —
I love Jesus, so do I,
I love Jesus, so do I,
I love Jesus, hallelujah,

I love Jesus, so do I,
I love Jesus, he's my Savior,
Jesus smiles and loves me too.

— 29 —

Even me, even me,
Let thy fullness fall on me;
Even me, even me,
Let thy fullness fall on me.

— 20 —
Oh, How I Love Jesus.

1 How sweet the name of Jesus sounds,
   In a believer's ear;
It soothes his sorrows, heals his wounds,
   And drives away his fear.

CHORUS.—Oh, how I love Jesus,
   Oh, how I love Jesus,
   Oh, how I love Jesus,
Because He first loved me.

2 It makes the wounded spirit whole,
   And calms the troubled breast;
'Tis manna to the hungry soul,
   And to the weary rest.

3 Dear Name, the rock on which I build—
   My shield and hiding place,
My never-failing treasure filled
   With boundless stores of grace.

4 I would thy boundless love proclaim,
   With ev'ry fleeting breath;

So shall the music of thy name
Refresh my soul in death.

— 21 —
Balm in Gilead.

1 How lost was my condition
   Till Jesus made me whole,
There is but one Physician
   Can cure a sin-sick soul.

Cho.—There's a balm in Gilead
    To make the wounded whole,
  There's power enough in Jesus
    To cure a sin-sick soul.

2 Next door to death he found me,
   And snatched me from the grave,
To tell to all around me
   His wondrous power to save.

3 The worst of all diseases
   Is light compared with sin ;
On every part it seizes,
   But rages most within.

4 'Tis palsy, plague, and fever,
   And madness, all combined ;
And none but a believer
   The least relief can find.

5 A dying, risen Jesus
   Seen by the eye of faith,
At once from danger frees us,
   And saves the soul from death.

6 Come then to this Physician,
   His help he'll freely give;
He makes no hard condition,
   'Tis only, Look and live.

— 22 —

Rejoicing in Entire Consecration.

1 Oh happy day that fixed my choice
   On Thee, my Savior and my God;
Well may this glowing heart rejoice,
   And tell its raptures all abroad.

Cho.—Happy day! Happy day!
   When Jesus washed my sins away,
   He taught me how to watch and pray,
   And live rejoicing every day.
     Happy day! Happy day!
   When Jesus washed my sins away.

2 Oh happy bond, that seals my vows
   To Him who merits all my love!
Let cheerful anthems fill the house,
   While to His altar now I move.

3 'Tis done—the great transaction's done;
   I am my Lord's and He is mine;
He drew me, and I followed on,
   Rejoiced to own the call divine.

4 Now rest—my long-divided heart—
   Fixed on this blissful center, rest—
Here have I found a nobler part,
   Here heavenly pleasures fill my breast.

Christian Warfare.

1 Am I a soldier of the cross?
   A follower of the Lamb?
   And shall I fear to own his cause,
   Or blush to speak his name?

2 Must I be carried to the skies,
   On flowery beds of ease,
   While others fought to win the prize,
   And sailed through bloody seas?

3 Are there no foes for me to face?
   Must I not stem the flood?
   Is this vile world a friend to grace?
   To help me on to God?

4 Sure I must fight, if I would reign;
   Increase my courage, Lord!
   I'll bear the toil, endure the pain,
   Supported by thy Word.

5 Thy saints in all this glorious war,
   Shall conquer, though they die;
   They see the triumph from afar,
   By faith they bring it nigh.

6 When that illustrious day shall rise,
   And all thy armies shine
   In robes of victory through the skies
   The glory shall be thine.

CHORUSES.

— 1 —

O, they look like men, yes, they look like men,
They look like men of war;
They are all dressed in uniform,
And conquering palms they bear.

— 2 —

I'd rather be the least of them
Who are the Lord's alone,
Than wear a royal diadem,
And sit upon a throne.

— 3 —

And when the war is over,
We shall wear a crown,
We shall wear a crown,
We shall wear a crown,
And when the war is over
We shall wear a crown
In the new Jerusalem.

— 24 —

Full Salvation.

1 Precious Savior thou hast saved me;
Thine, and only thine I am;
O! the cleansing blood has reached me,
Glory, glory to the Lamb.

Cho.—Glory, glory, Jesus saves me
Glory, glory to the Lamb;
O! the cleansing blood has reached me,
Glory, glory to the Lamb.

2 Long my yearning heart was trying
   To enjoy this perfect rest;
   But I gave all trying over:
   Simply trusting, I was blest.

3 Trusting, trusting every moment;
   Feeling now the blood applied;
   Lying at the cleansing fountain;
   Dwelling in my Savior's side.

4 Consecrated to thy service,
   I will live and die to Thee:
   I will witness to thy glory
   Of salvation full and free.

5 Yes, I will stand up for Jesus;
   He has sweetly saved my soul,
   Cleansed me from inbred corruption,
   Sanctified, and made me whole.

6 Glory to the blood that bought me!
   Glory to the cleansing power!
   Glory to the blood that keeps me!
   Glory, glory, evermore.

— 25 —
Angels Hovering Round.

There are angels hov'ring round,
There are angels hov'ring round,
There are angels hov'ring round.

‖: To carry the tidings home, :‖
‖: To the New Jerusalem, :‖
‖: Poor sinners are coming home, :‖
‖: And Jesus bids them come, :‖

‖: Let him that heareth come, :‖
‖: And he that is thirsty come, :‖
‖: And whosoever will may come, :‖
‖: There's glory all around. :‖

— 26 —

Longing to See Jesus.

1 Oh! when shall I see Jesus,
    And reign with Him above?
And drink the flowing fountain
    Of everlasting love?
When shall I be delivered
    From this vain world of sin;
And with my blessed Jesus
    Drink endless pleasure in?

2 But now I am a soldier,
    My Captain's gone before.
He's given me my orders,
    And tells me not to fear;
And if I hold out faithful,
    A crown of life He'll give,
And all His valiant soldiers
    Eternal life shall have.

3 Through grace I am determined
    To conquer though I die;
And then away to Jesus
    On wings of love I'll fly!
Farewell to sin and sorrow,
    I bid them all adieu;
And you my friends, prove faithful,
    And on your way pursue.

4 And if you meet with trials
    And troubles on your way,
Then cast your cares on Jesus,
    And don't forget to pray;
Gird on your heavenly armor
    Of hope and faith, and love;
And when your race is ended,
    You'll reign with Him above.

5 Oh, do not be discouraged,
    For Jesus is your friend:
And if you lack for knowledge,
    He'll not forget to lend:
Neither will He upbraid you,
    Though often you request;
He'll give you grace to conquer,
    And take you home to rest.

CHORUSES.

— 1 —

We will rise in the morning,
We will rise in the morning,
We will rise in the morning,
    To shout His praise on high.

— 2 —

We're coming ever nearer,
    Nearer, nearer,
We're coming ever nearer,
    To our eternal home.

— 3 —

O, how lovely, how lovely,
    How lovely, is Jesus,

He is my Redeemer,
   My Lord and my God.

— 4 —

We are bound for the kingdom,
We are bound for the kingdom,
We are bound for the kingdom,
   We are on our journey home.

— 5 —

When we meet on that shore,
When we meet on that shore,
When we meet on that shore,
   We shall live forever more.

— 6 —

Good news goes to Canaan,
Good news goes to Canaan,
Good news goes to Canaan,
   I'm on my way.

— 7 —

We're on our way to Zion,
We're on our way to Zion,
We're on our way to Zion,
   To the New Jerusalem.

— 8 —

Christ is all the world to me,
And His glory I shall see;
And before I'd leave my Savior,
I'd lay me down and die.

— 9 —

A few more days in the wilderness,
   Glory O, glory O,

A few more days in the wilderness,
    Glory hallelujah.

— 10 —

We're nearer, nearer home,
O blessed happy home!
Where grief and sin can never come,
Nearer to my happy home,
Nearer home, nearer home,
O blessed happy home.

— 11 —

Then palms of victory, crowns of glory,
    Palms of victory I shall wear.
Then palms of victory, crowns of glory,
    Palms of victory I shall wear.

— 27 —

The Penitent Inquirer.

1 Depth of mercy!—can there be
Mercy still reserved for me?
Can my God His wrath forbear,
Me the chief of sinners spare?

Cho.—God is love! I know, I feel:
    Jesus weeps and loves me still;
      Jesus weeps,
    He weeps, and loves me still.

2 I have long withstood His grace;
Long provoked Him to His face;
Would not hear His gracious calls,
Grieved Him by a thousand falls.

3 Jesus, answer from above;
   Is not all Thy nature love?
   Wilt Thou not the wrong forget,
   Lo, I fall before Thy feet.

4 Now incline me to repent;
   Let me now my fall lament;
   Deeply my revolt deplore;
   Weep, believe, and sin no more.

— 28 —

Hymn and Chorus.

1 We have brethren over yonder,
   We have brethren over yonder,
   We have brethren over yonder,
      In the New Jerusalem.

Cho.—By and by we'll go and see them,
   By and by we'll go and see them,
   By and by we'll go and see them,
      In the New Jerusalem.

2 We have sisters over yonder. :

3 We have brothers over yonder. :

4 We have children over yonder. :

5 We have fathers over yonder. :

6 We have mothers over yonder. :

7 We have kindred over yonder. :

8 We have Jesus over yonder. :

The Sweet Rest in Eden.

1 In the sweet fields of Eden,
  Over there, over there;
  In the sweet fields of Eden,
  Over there, over there.

Cho.—Over there, over there,
  Over there, over there,
  In the sweet fields of Eden,
  Over there.

2 There the tree of life is blooming. :

3 There is rest for the weary. :

4 On the other side of Jordan. :

5 You will never have a trial. :

6 Say, brother, will you meet me. :

7 By the grace of God I'll meet you. :

8 We will meet no more to sever. :

9 Then we'll wear our crowns of glory. :

10 And we'll walk and talk with Jesus. :

The Gospel Ship.

1 The Gospel Ship is sailing,
  Sailing, sailing;
  The Gospel Ship is sailing,
  Bound for Canaan's happy shore.

All who would ship for glory,
  Glory, glory;
All who would ship for glory,
  Come and welcome, rich and poor.

Cho.—Glory, hallelujah!
    All on board are sweetly singing;
  Glory, hallelujah!
    Hallelujah to the Lamb!

2 She has landed many thousands
    On fair Canaan's happy shore,
  And thousands now are sailing,
    Yet there's room for thousands more.

3 Sails filled with heavenly breezes,
    Swiftly glide the ship along,
  Her company are singing,
    Glory, glory is their song.

4 Take passage now for glory,
    Sailing o'er life's troubled sea,
  With us you shall be happy,
    Happy through eternity.

— 31 —

The Gate Ajar for Me.

1 There is a gate that stands ajar,
    And thro' its portals gleaming,
  A radiance from the cross afar
    The Savior's love revealing.

Ref.—O, depths of mercy! can it be
    That gate was left ajar for me?
      For me, for me?
    Was left ajar for me?

2 That gate ajar stands free for all
    Who seek through it salvation;
The rich and poor, the great and small,
    Of every tribe and nation.

3 Press onward then, tho' foes may frown,
    While mercy's gate is open,
Accept the cross and win the crown,
    Love's everlasting token.

4 Beyond the river's brink we'll lay
    The Cross that here is given,
And bear the Crown of life away,
    And love Him more in heaven.

— 32 —

The Heavenly Canaan.

1 There is a land of pure delight,
    Where saints immortal reign;
Eternal day excludes the night,
    And pleasures banish pain.

2 There everlasting spring abides,
    And never-withering flowers;
Death, like a narrow sea divides
    This heavenly land from ours.

3 Sweet fields beyond the swelling flood
    Stand dressed in living green;
So to the Jews old Canaan stood,
    While Jordan rolled between.

4 Could we but climb where Moses stood,
    And view the landscape o'er,

Not Jordan's stream, nor death's cold flood,
Should fright us from the shore.

— 33 —

Heaven in Prospect.

1 On Jordan's stormy banks I stand,
  And cast a wishful eye
To Canaan's fair and happy land,
  Where my possessions lie.

2 O the transporting rapt'rous scene,
  That rises to my sight!
Sweet fields arrayed in living green,
  And rivers of delight!

3 There generous fruits that never fail
  On trees immortal grow;
There rocks and hills, and brooks and vales
  With milk and honey flow.

4 All o'er these wide extended plains
  Shines one eternal day;
There God, the Sun, forever reigns
  And scatters night away.

5 No chilling winds, nor pois'nous breath
  Can reach that healthful shore;
Sickness and sorrow, pain and death,
  Are felt and feared no more.

6 When shall I reach that happy place,
  And be forever blest?
When shall I see my Father's face,
  And in His bosom rest.

CHORUSES.

— 1 —

I want to go, I want to go,
I want to go there too,
I want to go where Jesus is,
I want to go there too.

— 2 —

There's a better day, there's a crowning day,
There's a crowning day coming on,
Coming on, coming on,
There's a better day coming on.

— 3 —

Far away beyond the starlit skies,
Where the love light never, never dies,
Gleameth a mansion filled with delight,
Sweet, happy home so bright.

— 4 —

We shall rest in the fair and hapy land,
Just across on the evergreen shore,
Sing the song of Moses and the Lamb,
And dwell with Jesus evermore.

— 5 —

There you'll sing hallelujah
And I'll sing hallelujah,
And we'll all sing hallelujah,
In that bright world above.

— 6 —

Where the pearly gates shall never, never close,
And the tree of life its dewy shadow throws,
Where the ransomed ones in love repose,
Our glorious home shall be.

— 7 —

Then we'll sing hallelujah to God and the Lamb,
  Who has saved us from our sorrow and pain,
Yes, we'll sing hallelujah to God and the Lamb,
  When we meet on the bright golden plain.

— 8 —

O home, sweet home, sweet home,
I am sighing and longing for home;
Beyond the pearly gates many mansions wait
For the weary ones who journey home.

— 9 —

O come angel band,
Come and around me stand,
O bear me away on your snowy wings
To my eternal home,
O bear me away on your snowy wings
To my eternal home.

— 10 —

We'll shout his praise in glory,
  So will I! so will I!
And we'll all sing Hallelujah
  In heaven by-and-by.

— 34 —

That Beautiful Land.

1 A beautiful land by faith I see,
  A land of rest, from sorrow free;
  The house of the ransomed, bright and fair,
  And beautiful angels, too, are there.

CHORUS.—Will you go? will you go? go to that
 beautiful land with me?
 Will you go? will you go? go to that
 beautiful land?

2 That land is called the City of Light;
It ne'er has known the shades of night!
The glory of God, the light of day,
Hath driven the darkness far away.

3 In vision I see its streets of gold,
Its gates of pearl too I behold;
The river of life, the crystal sea,
The ambrosial fruit of life's fair tree.

4 The ransomed throng, arrayed in white,
In rapture range the plains of light;
In one harmonious choir they praise
Their glorious Savior's matchless grace.

— 35 —
Christ.

1 Rock of ages, cleft for me,
Let me hide myself in thee;
Let the water and the blood,
From thy side a healing flood,
Be of sin the double cure,—
Save from wrath and make me pure.

2 Should my tears forever flow,
Sould my zeal no languor know!
All for sin could not atone;
Thou must save, and thou alone;
In my hands no price I bring;
Simply to thy cross I cling.

3 While I draw this fleeting breath,
   When my eyes shall close in death,
   When I rise to worlds unknown,
   See thee on thy judgment throne—
   Rock of ages, cleft for me,
   Let me hide myself in thee.

— 36 —

Praise Before and After Death.

1 I'm glad that I was born to die;
   From grief and woe my soul shall fly;
   Bright angels shall convey me home,
   Away to the New Jerusalem.

2 I'll praise my Maker while I've breath;
   I hope to praise Him after death;
   I hope to praise Him when I die,
   And shout salvation as I fly.

3 Farewell vain world, I'm going home,
   My Savior smiles and bids me come;
   Sweet angels beckon me away;
   To sing God's praise in endless day.

4 I soon shall pass the vail of death,
   And in His arm's I'll lose my breath!
   And then my happy soul shall tell,
   My Jesus hath done all things well.

5 When to that blessed world I rise,
   And join the anthems in the skies,
   This note above the rest shall swell
   My Jesus has done all things well.

6 Then shall I see my gracious God,
And praise Him in His bright abode,
My theme through all eternity,
Shall glory, glory, glory, glory be.

CHORUSES.

— 1 —

O let me in thy kingdom,
O let me in thy kingdom,
O let me in thy kingdom,
I am on my way.

— 2 —

I've given my heart to Jesus,
Happy am I, happy am I,
I've given my heart to Jesus,
Happy am I to-day.

— 3 —

I am happy now and I know I shall be,
When my friends in glory I'll see,
I'm happy, happy,
May the Lord continue with me.

— 4 —

Glory to God!
We're at the fountain drinking,
Glory to God!
We're on our journey home.

— 5 —

O Lord! bless my soul,
And I'll shout glory,
And when I die convey me home,
And I'll shout glory.

— 6 —

We'll cross the river of Jordan,
    Happy, happy,
We'll cross the river of Jordan,
    Happy in the Lord.

— 7 —

Praise the Lord, O my soul,
    Glory, Hallelujah,
Praise the Lord, O my soul,
    Praise ye the Lord.

— 8 —

My soul is heaven bound,
    Halle, O Hallelujah,
My soul is heaven bound,
    Praise ye the Lord.

— 9 —

Happy land, happy land,
    Happy land of rest,
Sweet Canaan, sweet Canaan,
    Happy land of rest.

— 10 —

In the morning, in the morning of the Lord,
    And we'll all rise together in the morning,
In the morning, in the morning of the Lord,
    And we'll all rise together in the morning.

— 11 —

We're going to Zion,
    Halle, O Hallelujah,
We're going to the New Jerusalem,
    Halle, O Hallelujah.

― 12 ―

Glory hallelujah,
Praise Him, hallelujah,
Glory hallelujah,
Praise ye the Lord.

― 13 ―

O Canaan, sweet Canaan,
I'm bound for the land of Canaan,
O Canaan, it is my happy home,
I'm bound for the land of Canaan.

― 14 ―

There's one more river
And that's the river of Jordan,
There's one more river
There's one more river to cross.

― 15 ―

For we have a right up yonder,
In the New Jerusalem,
For we have a right up yonder,
Hallelujah.

― 16 ―

We've been waiting to go,
We've been waiting to go,
We've been waiting to go,
Over in Glory.

― 17 ―

There's a better day a coming,
Come and go along with me,
There's a better day a coming,
Go sound the Jubilee.

— 18 —

Glory be to the Lord on high,
  He who reigns above the sky,
He's promised me if I'd faithful be,
  I shall reign with him in Glory.

— 19 —

I hope to die in the field of battle,
And I hope to die in the field of battle,
And I hope to die in the field of battle,
  With the Glory in my soul.

— 20 —

We're going home, we're going home,
  We're going home, to die no more,
To die no more, to die no more,
  We're going home, to die no more.

— 21 —

Jesus, Jesus,
All the way 'long it is Jesus,
Jesus, Jesus,
All the way 'long it is Jesus.

— 22 —

O, heaven is my home,
  My journey I'll pursue,
I never will turn back,
  While heaven's in my view.

— 23 —

There is joy in heaven, and I feel it in my soul,
  And I love God, Glory Hallelujah;
There is joy in heaven, and I feel it in my soul,
  Aud I love God, Glory Hallelujah.

— 24 —

All my days living in the kingdom,
All my days living in the kingdom,
All my days living in the kingdom,
Looking at the dying Lamb.

— 25 —

Home, home, home is so sweet,
We're going to Jesus,
His name is so sweet.

— 26 —

Oh, he's taken my feet from the mire and the clay,
And he's placed them on the rock of ages.

— 27 —

Play on the golden harp,
Yes, play on the golden harp,
I want to go where Jesus is,
And play on a golden harp.

— 37 —

The Highway of Holiness.

1 Jesus my all to heaven is gone—
He, whom I fix my hopes upon;
His track I see, and I'll pursue
The narrow way, till Him I view.

2 The way the holy prophets went,—
The roads that leads from banishment,
The King's highway of holiness,
I'll go, for all His paths are peace.

3 This is the way I long have sought
And mourn'd because I found it not;
My grief a burden long has been,
Because I was not saved from sin.

4 The more I strove against its power,
I felt its weight and guilt the more;
Till late I heard my Savior say,—
Come hither, soul, I am the way.

5 Lo! glad I come; and thou, blest Lamb,
Shall take me to Thee, as I am;
Nothing but sin have I to give,—
Nothing but love shall I receive.

6 Then will I tell to sinners round,
What a dear Savior I have found,
I'll point to Thy redeeming blood,
And say—behold the way to God.

CHORUSES.

— 1 —

O mourning souls, come along,
Jesus is the way,
O mourning souls, come along,
Jesus is the way.

— 2 —

Wrestle on, wrestle on,
You shall gain the victory,
Wrestle on, wrestle on,
You shall gain the day.

— 3 —

Away down in the valley hear me cry,
   Give me Jesus, or I die,
Away down in the valley, hear me cry,
   Give me Jesus or I die.

— 4 —

Come to the Savior, come,
   Come to the Savior now,
His wounds for you stand open wide,
   Come to the Savior, come.

— 5 —

Sing on, pray on, we're gaining ground,
   Halle, O Hallelujah,
The power of the Lord is coming down,
   Halle, O Hallelujah.

— 6 —

Amen, amen, my Jesus is coming,
   O, Halle, O, Halle, Hallelujah,
Amen, amen, my Jesus is coming,
   O, Halle, O, Halle, Hallelujah.

— 7 —

Higher than I, higher than I,
O, lead me to the Rock that is higher than I;
   Higher than I, higher than I,
O, lead me to the Rock that is higher than I.

— 8 —

O! only believe and trust in God,
   For Jesus has died to save you,
O! only believe and trust in God,
   For Jesus has died to save you.

— 9 —

Save, O, save, save, my dear Savior,
And send converting power down,
Save, my dear Lord.

— 10 —

O Lord! send us a blessing,
O Lord! send us a blessing,
O Lord! send us a blessing,
O! send us a blessing from heaven above.

— 11 —

O, if there's any mercy, Lord,
Send it down to me,
O, Halle, Halle, Hallelujah.

— 12 —

I'm so glad Jesus came the world to save,
I'm so glad, He came to save me;
I'm so glad Jesus came the world to save,
I'm so glad, He came to save me.

— 13 —

There is a resting place,
There is a resting place,
There is a resting place,
For the people of God.

— 14 —

We'll wait till Jesus comes,
We'll wait till Jesus comes,
We'll wait till Jesus comes,
And we'll be gathered home.

— 15 —

O, will you, will you, will you come to the cross,
Will you come to the cross
I have died on for you,
To save you from sin, and to save you from woe.

— 16 —

Sinner, O, sinner, give your heart to God,
For soon the reaping time will come,
Give your heart to God,
The angels shout the harvest home,
Give your heart to God,
Sinner, O, sinner, give your heart to God.

— 17 —

O, repent, poor sinner, O, repent, poor sinner,
For you'll wish you had repented when you die,
O, repent poor sinner, O, repent, poor sinner,
For you'll wish you had repented when you die.

— 18 —

Happy on the way, happy on the way,
Bless the Lord, I'm happy on the way.

— 19 —

Ho every one that thirsts!
Come ye to the waters,
Freely drink and quench your thirst,
Zion's sons and daughters.

— 20 —

To-day you'd better repent,
To-morrow you may die,
To-day you'd better repent,
To-morrow you may die.

— 21 —

The Lamb! the Lamb! the bleeding Lamb!
I love the sound of Jesus' name,
It sets my spirit all aflame,
   Glory to the bleeding Lamb!

— 22 —

Give me Jesus, give me Jesus,
   You may have all this world,
      Give me Jesus.

— 23 —

I know that my Redeemer lives,
   Glory, Hallelujah!
What joy this blest assurance gives,
   Praise ye the Lord.

— 24 —

Hallelujah! Hallelujah!
We're a happy little band, Hallelujah!
Hallelujah! Hallelujah!
We're a happy little band, Hallelujah!

— 25 —

Don't talk about troubles here below,
   But talk about lovely Jesus;
Don't talk about troubles here below,
   But talk about lovely Jesus.

— 26 —

We'll join the pilgrim band,
   And on to glory go,
We're traveling to a better land
   Our home is not below.

— 27 —

I will go to Jesus,
I will go to Jesus,
I will go to Jesus,
And be saved.

— 28 —

O sinner, O sinner, you'd better begin,
Better begin, better begin!
The door will be shut and you cannot get in;
O what will you do in that day?

— 29 —

I'm saved, I am, I know I am,
I'm washed in Jesus' blood,
I'm saved, I am, I know I am,
I'm washed in Jesus' blood,
I'm saved, I am, I know I am,
I'm washed in Jesus' blood,
And the Lord has pardoned all my sins.

— 30 —

Eternal life, eternal life,
We have it in the Savior;
Eternal life, eternal life,
We have it in the Savior.

— 38 —

The Great Physician.

1 The great Physician now is near,
The sympathising Jesus;
He speaks the drooping heart to cheer,
O, hear the voice of Jesus.

CHORUS.—Sweetest note in seraph song,
Sweetest name on mortal tongue,
Sweetest carol ever sung,
Jesus, blessed Jesus.

2 Your many sins are all forgiven,
O, hear the voice of Jesus;
Go on your way in peace to heaven,
And wear a crown with Jesus.

3 All glory to the dying Lamb!
I now believe in Jesus;
I love the blessed Savior's name.
I love the name of Jesus.

4 Come, brethren, help me sing His praise,
O, praise the name of Jesus;
Come, sisters, all your voices raise,
O, bless the name of Jesus.

— 39 —

Why Do You Wait?

1 Why do you wait, dear brother,
O, why do you tarry so long?
Your Savior is waiting to give you
A place in His sanctified throng.

CHORUS.—Why not? why not?
Why not come to Him now?
Why not? why not?
Why not come to Him now?

2 What do you hope, dear brother,
To gain by a further delay?

There's no one to save you but Jesus,
　　There's no other way but His way.

3 Do you not feel, dear brother,
　　His Spirit now striving within?
　O, why not accept His salvation,
　　And throw off thy burden of sin?

4 Why do you wait, dear brother?
　　The harvest is passing away,
　Your Savior is longing to bless you,
　　There's danger and death in delay.

— 40 —
Wonderful Words of Life.

1 Sing them over again to me,
　　Wonderful words of Life.
　Let me more of their beauty see,
　　Wonderful words of Life.
　Words of life and beauty,
　Teach me faith and duty;
　Beautiful words, wonderful words,
　Wonderful words of Life.

2 Christ the blessed One gives to all
　　Wonderful words of Life;
　Sinner, list to the loving call,
　　Wonderful words of Life.
　All so freely given,
　Wooing us to heaven,
　Beautiful words, wonderful words,
　Wonderful words of Life.

3 Sweetly echo the gospel call,
　　Wonderful words of Life,

Offer pardon and peace to all,
  Wonderful words of Life.
Jesus, only Savior,
Sanctify forever,
Beautiful words, wonderful words,
Wonderful words of Life.

— 41 —

Is My Name Written There?

1 Lord, I care not for riches,
    Neither silver nor gold;
  I would make sure of heaven,
    I would enter the fold,
  In the book of the kingdom,
    With its pages so fair,
  Tell me, Jesus, my Savior,
    Is my name written there?

Cho.—Is my name written there,
    On the page white and fair?
  In the book of Thy kingdom,
    Is my name written there?

2 Lord, my sins they are many,
    Like the sands of the sea;
  But Thy blood, O, my Savior!
    Is sufficient for me;
  For Thy promise is written,
    In bright letters that glow,
  "Though your sins be as scarlet,
    I will make them like snow."

3 O, that beautiful city,
    With its mountains of light,

With its glorified beings,
   In pure garments of white;
Where no evil thing cometh,
   To despoil what is fair;
Where the angels are watching—
   Is my name written there?

— 42 —

Nearer, My God, to Thee.

1 Nearer, my God, to thee,
    Nearer to thee!
E'en though it be a cross
    That raiseth me;
Still all my song shall be,
Nearer, my God, to thee,
    Nearer to thee!

2 Though like a wanderer,
    The sun gone down,
Darkness comes over me,
    My rest a stone;
Yet in my dreams I'd be
Nearer, my God, to thee,
    Nearer to thee.

3 There let my way appear
    Steps up to heaven;
All that thou sendest me
    In mercy given;
Angels to beckon me
Nearer, my God, to thee!
    Nearer to thee.

Unwearied Earnestness.

1 Father, I stretch my hands to Thee;
   No other help I know:
 If Thou withdraw Thyself from me,
   Ah! whither shall I go?

2 What did Thine only Son endure,
   Before I drew my breath?
 What pain, what labor, to secure
   My soul from endless death.

3 O Jesus, could I this believe,
   I now should feel its power;
 And all my wants Thou wouldst relieve,
   In this accepted hour.

4 Author of faith! to Thee I lift
   My weary, longing eyes:
 O let me now receive that gift,—
   My soul without it dies.

5 Surely Thou canst not let me die;
   O speak, and I shall live,
 And here I will unwearied lie,
   Till Thou thy Spirit give.

6 How would my fainting soul rejoice,
   Could I but see Thy face;
 Now let me hear Thy quick'ning voice,
   And taste Thy pard'ning grace.

CHORUS.

We're kneeling at a throne of grace,
Throne of grace, throne of grace,
We're kneeling at a throne of grace,
Where God will answer prayer.

— 44 —

The Presence of Jesus Desired.

1 How tedious and tasteless the hours,
When Jesus no longer I see!
Sweet prospects, sweet birds, and sweet flowers
Have lost all their sweetness to me:
The midsummer sun shines but dim;
The fields strive in vain to look gay,
But when I am happy in Him,
December's as pleasant as May.

2 His name yields the richest perfume,
And sweeter than music his voice;
His presence disperses my gloom,
And makes all within me rejoice:
I should, were he always so nigh,
Have nothing to wish or to fear;
No mortal so happy as I;
My summer would last all the year.

3 Content with beholding his face,
My all to his pleasure resigned,
No changes of season or place
Would make any change in my mind:
While blest with a sense of his love,
A palace a toy would appear;
And prisons would palaces prove,
If Jesus would dwell with me there.

4 Dear Lord, if indeed I am thine,
    If thou art my sun and my song,
Say, why do I languish and pine?
    And why are my winters so long?
O, drive these dark clouds from sky;
    Thy soul-cheering presence restore;
Or take me to thee up on high,
    Where winter and clouds are no more.

— 45 —

Home Beyond the Tide.

1 We are out on the ocean sailing,
    Homeward bound we sweetly glide,
We are out on the ocean sailing,
    To our home beyond the tide.

Cho.—All the storms will soon be over,
    Then we'll anchor in the harbor,
We are out on the ocean sailing,
    To our home beyond the tide.

2 Millions now are safely landed
    Over on the golden shore;
Millions more are on their journey,
    Yet there's room for millions more.

3 Come on board, oh ship for glory,
    Be in haste, make up your mind,
For your vessel's weighing anchor,
    You will soon be left behind.

4 When we all are safely anchor'd,
    We will shout our journey o'er;
We will walk about the city,
    And will sing forevermore.

Hallowed Spot.

1 There is a spot to me more dear
    Than native vale or mountain;
A spot for which affection's tear
    Springs grateful from its fountain:
'Tis not where kindred souls abound,
    Tho' that on earth is Heaven;
But where I first my Savior found,
    And felt my sins forgiven.

2 Hard was my toil to reach the shore,
    Long toss'd upon the ocean;
Above me was the thunder's roar;
    Beneath the waves' commotion:
Darkly the pall of night was thrown
    Around me, faint with terror;
In that dark hour—how did my groan
    Ascend for years of error!

3 Sinking and panting as for breath,
    I knew not help was near me;
And cried, "O! save me, Lord from death,
    Immortal Jesus, hear me."
Then quick as thought I felt him mine,
    My Savior stood before me;
I saw his brightness round me shine,
    And shouted, "Glory! Glory!"

4 Oh, sacred hour! oh, hallowed spot!
    Were love divine first found me;
Wherever falls my distant lot,
    My heart shall linger round thee;
And when from earth I rise to soar
    Up to my home in heaven,

Down will I cast my eyes once more,
Where I wast first forgiven.

— 47 —
On the Hills of Glory.

1 Look ye saints, and see the light,
   Over the hills of glory,
 Lo, the dawn is breaking bright,
   Over on the hills of glory.

Cho.—Bright crowns the saints shall wear,
    In yonder home so fair;
  O may we all meet there,
    Over on the fields of glory.

2 We shall meet on that bright shore,
   Over on the fields of glory;
 Meet with loved ones gone before;
   Over on the fields of glory.

3 We shall see the Savior there,
   Over on the hills of glory;
 And a crown of life shall wear,
   Over on the hills of glory.

4 O, the rest will be so sweet,
   Over on the hills of glory,
 When our journey is complete,
   Over on the hills of glory.

— 48 —
A Poor Sinner Saved.

1 I was once far away from my Savior,
   And as vile as a sinner could be,
 But I wondered if Christ, the Redeemer,
   Would save a poor sinner like me.

2 I wandered on in darkness,
    Not a ray of light could I see,
And the thought filled my heart with sadness,
    There's no hope for a sinner like me.

3 But then in that dark, lonely hour;
    A voice sweetly whispered to me,
Saying, "Christ, the Redeemer, hath power,
    To save a poor sinner like thee."

4 I then fully trusted in Jesus,
    And O what a joy came to me!
And now to others I'm telling,
    How he saved a poor sinner like me.

5 And when life's journey is ended,
    And I the dear Savior shall see;
I'll praise him forever and ever,
    For saving a sinner like me.

— 49 —

The Christian Life.

1 I am coming to the cross;
    I am poor and weak and blind;
I am counting all my dross,
    I shall full salvation find.

Cho.—I am trusting, Lord in Thee,
    Blest Lamb of Calvary;
    Humbly at thy cross I bow,
    Save me Jesus, save me now.

2 Long my heart has sighed for Thee,
    Long has evil reigned within;
Jesus sweetly speaks to me,—
    "I will cleanse you from all sin."

3 Here I give my all to Thee,
    Friends, and time, and earthly store;
Soul and body, Thine to be,—
    Wholly Thine forevermore.

4 In the promises I trust;
    Now I feel the blood applied,
I am prostrate in the dust;
    I with Christ am crucified.

5 Jesus comes! he fills my soul!
    Perfected in love I am!
I am every whit made whole;
    Glory! glory to the Lamb.

— 50 —

I Need Thee Every Hour.

1 I need thee every hour,
    Most gracious Lord;
No tender voice like thine
    Can peace afford.

REF.—I need thee, oh! I need thee;
    Every hour I need thee;
O bless me now, my Savior!
    I come to thee.

2 I need thee every hour;
    Stay thou near by;
Temptations lose their pow'r
    When thou art nigh.

3 I need thee every hour,
    In joy or pain;
Come quickly and abide,
    Or life is vain.

4 I need thee every hour;
   Teach me thy will;
   And thy rich promises
   In me fulfil.

5 I need thee every hour,
   Most Holy One;
   Oh, make me thine indeed,
   Thou blessed Son.

— 51 —
Take Me as I Am.

1 Just as I am, without one plea,
  But that thy blood was shed for me,
  And that thou bid'st me come to thee,
     O Lamb of God I come.

Cho.—Take me as I am, and waiting not
        O, bring thy free salvation nigh,
        And take me as I am.

2 Just as I am, and waiting not
  To rid my soul of one dark blot,
  To Thee, whose blood can cleanse each spot,
     O Lamb of God I come.

3 Just as I am, though tossed about
  With many a conflict, many a doubt,
  Fightings within, and fears without,
     O Lamb of God I come.

4 Just as I am, poor, wretched, blind;
  Sight, riches, healing of the mind,
  Yea, all I want, in Thee to find,
     O Lamb of God, I come.

5 Just as I am thou wilt receive,
　Wilt welcome, pardon, cleanse, relieve :
　Because thy promise I believe,
　　　O Lamb of God, I come.

6 Just as I am, thy love unknown
　Hath broken every barrier down ;
　Now to be thine, and thine alone,
　　　O Lamb of God, I come.

Cho.—We're kneeling at the mercy seat :
　Where Jesus answers prayers.

— 52 —

Pass Me Not.

1 Pass me not, O gentle Savior,
　　Hear my humble cry ;
　While on others Thou art smiling,
　　Do not pass me by.

Cho.—Savior, Savior,
　　　Hear my humble cry ;
　While on others Thou art calling,
　　Do not pass me by.

2 Let me at a throne of mercy
　　Find a sweet relief,
　Kneeling there in deep contrition,
　　Help my unbelief.

3 Trusting only in Thy merits,
　　Would I seek Thy face ;
　Heal my wounded, broken spirit,
　　Save me by Thy grace.

4 Thou, the spring of all my comfort
    More than life to me,
Whom have I on earth beside thee,
    Whom in heaven but thee.

— 53 —
Rain, O, Rain.

1 Rain, O rain, rain my dear Savior,
Rain, O rain, the Lord send it down,
Send the sanctifying power in the army of the Lord,
Send the sanctifying power in the army.

If my brother wants a blessing,
Why don't he come along?
He may pray and be as happy,
    In the army.

    If my sister wants a blessing.

    If my neighbor wants a blessing.

    If the mourner wants a blessing.

— 54 —
Over There.

1 Oh, think of a home over there,
    By the side of the river of light,
Where the saints, all immortal and fair,
    Are robed in their garments of white.

REFRAIN.—Over there, Over there,
    Oh, think of a home over there,
        Over there, Over there,
    Oh, think of a home over there.

2 Oh, think of the friends over there,
   Who before us the journey have trod,
Of the songs that they breathe on the air,
   In their home in the palace of God,
     Over there,
Oh, think of the friends over there.

3 My Savior is now over there,
   There my kindred and friends are at rest:
Then away from my sorrow and care,
   Let me fly to the land of the blest,
     Over there,
My Savior is now over there.

4 I'll soon be at home over there,
   For the end of my journey I see,
Many dear to my heart, over there,
   Are watching and waiting for me,
     Over there,
I'll soon be at home over there.

— 55 —
Portuguese Hymn.

1 How firm a foundation, ye saints of the Lord,
Is laid for your faith in his excellent word!
What more can he say than to you he hath said,
You, who unto Jesus for refuge have fled.

2 In every condition, in sickness, in health,
In poverty's vale, or abounding in wealth;
At home and abroad, on the land, on the sea,
As thy days may demand, shall thy strength ever be.

3 "Fear not, I am with thee, Oh! be not dismayed,
For I am thy God, and still will give thee aid;

    I'll strengthen thee, help thee, and cause thee to stand,
Upheld by my right'ous, omnipotent hand.

4 When thro' the deep waters I call thee to go,
The rivers of woe shall not thee overflow,
For I will be with thee, thy troubles to bless,
And sanctify to thee, thy deepest distress.

5 When thro' fiery trials thy pathway shall lie,
My grace all sufficient shall be thy supply;
The flames shall not hurt thee, I only design,
Thy dross to consume, and thy gold to refine.

6 Even down to old age, all my people shall prove,
My sov'reign, eternal, unchangeable love,
And when hoary hairs shall these temples adorn,
Like lambs they shall still in my bosom be borne.

7 "The soul that on Jesus doth lean for repose,
I will not, I will not desert to his foes;
That soul, tho' all hell should endeavor to shake,
I'll never—no never—no never forsake."

Sure Foundation.

1 My hope is built on nothing less
Then Jesus' blood and righteousness,
I dare not trust the sweetest frame,
But wholly lean on Jesus' name.

    On Christ the solid rock I stand;
    All other ground is sinking sand.

2 When darkness seems to veil his face,
  I rest on His unchanging grace;
  In every high and stormy gale
  My anchor holds within the veil.

3 His oath, his covenant and blood,
  Support me in the 'whelming flood:
  When all around my soul gives way,
  He then is all my hope and stay.

— 57 —
Rest in the Arms of Jesus.

1 Say, dear fathers, don't you want to go?
  Say, dear fathers, don't you want to go?
  Say, dear fathers, don't you want to go?
  And rest in the arms of Jesus.

Cho.—Yes, all together we will go,
  Yes, all together we will go,
  Yes, all together we will go,
  And rest in the arms of Jesus,

2 Say, dear mothers, don't you want to go?

3 Say, dear brothers, don't you want to go?

4 Say, dear sisters, don't you want to go?

5 Say, dear children, don't you want to go?

6 Say, dear neighbors, don't you want to go?

— 58 —
Whiter Than Snow.

1 Dear Jesus, I long to be perfectly whole;
  I want Thee forever to live in my soul;
  Break down every idol, cast out every foe;
  Now wash me and I shall be whiter than snow.

CHO.—Whiter than snow, yes whiter than snow,
　　　Now wash me and I shall be whiter than snow.

2　Dear Jesus come down from Thy throne in the skies,
　And help me to make a complete sacrifice;
　I give up myself, and whatever I know—
　Now wash me, and I shall be whiter than snow.

3　Dear Jesus, for this I most humbly entreat;
　I wait blessed Lord, at Thy crucified feet,
　By faith, for my cleansing, I see Thy blood flow,
　Now wash me, and I shall be whiter than snow.

4　The blessing of faith I receive from above;
　O glory! my soul is made perfect in love;
　My prayer has prevailed, and this moment I know,
　The blood is applied, I am whiter than snow.

— 59 —
Arise, My Soul Arise.

1　Arise, my soul arise;
　　Shake off thy guilty fears;
　The bleeding sacrifice
　　In my behalf appears;
‖: Before the throne my surety stands, :‖
　My name is written on His hands.

2　He ever lives above,
　　For me to intercede,
　His all redeeming love,
　　His precious blood to plead;
‖: His blood atoned for all our race, :‖
　And sprinkles now the throne of grace.

3 Five bleeding wounds He bears,
  Received on Calvary;
 They pour effectual prayers,
  They strongly plead for me;
‖: Forgive him, oh, forgive they cry, :‖
 Nor let that randsomed sinner die.

4 My God is reconciled;
  His pardoning voice I hear;
 He owns me for His child;
  I can no longer fear;
‖: With confidence I now draw nigh, :‖
 And Father, Abba, Father cry.

— 60 —
Over Yonder.

1 My father's gone to view that land,
 To view that land, to view that land,
My father's gone to view that land,
 To sing that cheering song.

  Cho.—Away over yonder,
   Along side of Jordan,
  Away over yonder,
   To sing that cheering song.

2 My mother's gone to view that land. :

3 My brother's gone to view that land. :

4 My sister's gone to view that land. :

5 My children are gone to view that land. :

6 My friends are gone to view that land. :

Zion's Travelers.

1 Children of the heavenly King,
As we journey let us sing;
Sing our Savior's worthy praise,
Glorious in his works and ways.

2 We are trav'ling home to God,
In the way our fathers trod;
They are happy now, and we
Soon their happiness shall see.

3 O ye banished seed be glad;
Christ our Advocate is made;
Us to save our flesh assumes,—
Brother to our souls becomes.

4 Fear not, brethren, joyful stand
On the borders of the land;
Jesus Christ our Father's Son,
Bids us undismayed go on.

5 Lord! obediently we'll go,
Gladly leaving all below;
Only thou our leader be,
And we still will follow thee.

CHORUSES.

— 1 —

Let us walk in the light,
In the light, in the light,
Let us walk in the light,
In the light of God.

— 2 —

Looking home, looking home,
    Toward the heavenly mansions,
Jesus hath prepared for me,
    In my Father's kingdom.

— 3 —

Praise the Lord, praise the Lord,
O, he died for you and me, praise the Lord,
    Yes, he died for you and me
    On the mount of Calvary,
Yes, he died for you and me, praise the Lord.

— 4 —

Happy on the way, happy on the way,
Bless the Lord, I'm happy on the way.

— 62 —
Our Refuge.

1 Jesus, lover of my soul,
    Let me to Thy bosom fly,
  While the nearer waters roll,
    While the tempest still is high;
  Hide me, oh, my Savior, hide,
    Till the storm of life is past;
  Safe into the heaven guide,
    Oh, receive my soul at last.

2 Other refuge have I none,
    Hangs my helpless soul on Thee;
  Leave, oh, leave me not alone,
    Still support and comfort me.
  All my trust in Thee is stayed,
    All my help from Thee I bring;

  Cover my defenceless head
   With the shadow of Thy wing.

3 Thou, O Christ, art all I want,
  More than all in Thee I find ;
 Raise the fallen, cheer the faint,
  Heal the sick and lead the blind.
 Just and holy is Thy name ;
  I am all unrighteousness ;
 False and full of sin I am,
  Thou art full of truth and grace.

4 Plenteous grace with Thee is found,
  Grace to cover all my sin ;
 Let the healing streams abound ;
  Make and keep me pure within.
 Thou of life the fountain art ;
  Freely let me take of Thee ;
 Spring Thou up within my heart ;
  Rise to all eternity.

CHORUS.

Jesus is a rock in a weary land,
 Weary land, weary land ;
Jesus is a rock in a weary land,
 A shelter in a time of storm.

— 63 —

In the Sweet By-and-By.

1 There's a land that is fairer than day,
 And by faith we can see it afar :
For the Father waits over the way,
 To prepare us a dwelling place there.

Cho.—In the sweet by-and-by
    We shall meet on that beautiful shore.
In the sweet by-and-by,
    We shall meet on that beautiful shore.

2 We shall sing on that beautiful shore,
    The melodious songs of the blest;
And our spirits shall sorrow no more,
    Nor sigh for the blessing of rest.

3 To our bountiful Father above,
    We will offer the tribute of praise,
For the glorious gift of his love,
    And the blessings that hallow our days.

4 We shall rest on that beautiful shore,
    In the joys of the sav'd we shall share;
All our pilgrimage-toil will be o'er,
    And the conqueror's crown we shall wear.

5 We shall meet, we shall sing, we shall reign
    In the land where the saved never die!
We shall rest free from sorrow and pain,
    Safe at home in the sweet by-and-by.

INDEX.

FIRST LINES.   **NO.**

A beautiful land by faith I see, ...34
A charge to keep I have, ...13
Alas and did my Savior bleed, ...9
Almost persuaded, now to believe, ...5
Am I a soldier of the cross, ...23
And must I be to judgment brought, ...18
Arise, my soul, arise, ...59

Behold a stranger at the door, ...1

Children of the heavenly king, ...61
Come, sinners, to the gospel feast, ...3
Come thou fount of every blessing, ...19
Come to Jesus, come to Jesus, ...6
Come we that love the Lord, ...15
Come, ye sinners, poor and needy, ...2

Depths of mercy! can there be, ...27
Dear Jesus, I long to be perfectly whole, ...58
Down at the cross where my Savior died, ...4

Father, I stretch my hands to thee, ...43

How firm a foundation, ye saints of the Lord, ...55
How lost was my condition, ...21
How sweet the name of Jesus sounds, ...20
How tedious and tasteless the hours, ...44

I am coming to the cross, ...49
I gave my life for thee, ...11
I'm glad that I was born to die, ...56
I need thee every hour, ...50
In the Christian's home in glory, ...16
In the sweet fields of Eden, ...29
I was once far away from my Savior, ...48

Jesus, lover of my soul, ...62
Jesus my all to heaven is gone, ...37

Title	Page
Just as I am, without one plea,	51
Look ye saints, and see the light,	47
Lord, I care not for riches,	41
My father's gone to view that land,	60
My hope is built on nothing less,	56
Nearer, my God, to thee	42
Not all the blood of beasts,	15
O, come to-day to the fountain,	8
O, come to the Savior to-day,	7
O, happy day, that fixed my choice,	22
O, think of a home over there,	54
O, when shall I see Jesus,	26
On Jordan's stormy banks I stand,	33
Pass me not, O gentle Savior,	52
Precious Savior, thou hast saved us	24
Rain, O rain my dear Savior,	53
Rock of ages, cleft for me,	35
Say, dear fathers, don't you want to go,	57
Sing them over again to me,	40
The gospel ship is sailing,	30
The great Physician now is near,	38
The judgment day is coming,	12
There are angels hovering round,	25
There is a fountain filled with blood,	10
There is a gate that stands ajar,	31
There is a land of pure delight,	32
There is a spot to me more dear,	46
There's a land that is fairer than day,	63
We are out on the ocean sailing,	45
We have brethren over yonder,	28
What can wash away my stain,	17
Why do you wait, dear brother,	39

P. WIEST'S SONS'
New Store,

10 W. Market Street,

YORK, PENN'A.,

You will always find a full line of all kinds of

Dry Goods

AND

Notions,

Best in the City,

AT THE LOWEST PRICES.

SUBSCRIBE FOR
The True Believer!

AN OCTAVO MONTHLY DEVOTED TO

Vital Godliness.

This is a safe Magazine for all classes, and ought to find a place in every home.

IT IS

Evangelical,
Undenominational,
Devotional.

SUBSCRIPTION PRICE—50 Cents per Year in Advance.

EDITORS AND PUBLISHERS:

Rev. I. H. ALBRIGHT,
Rev. C. A. BURTNER, } York, Pa.

Address either of the above.

ARTHUR P. ROSSER,

ARCHITECT,

8 West Market Street,

YORK, PENN'A.

Consulting Engineer for Sanitary Works.

R. F. POLACK,

DEALER IN

Watches, Jewelry, Silverware, Diamonds, Fine China and Spectacles.

—

EYES EXAMINED FREE OF CHARGE.

—

Opposite the Court House, York, Pa.

YOU ALWAYS FIND THE
Largest and Best
SELECTED STOCK
OF
READY-MADE
Clothing
—AND—
Gents' Furnishing Goods,
—AT—
LEHMAYER & BRO.,
THE OLD AND RELIABLE,
5 E. Market Street, York, Pa.

HEADQUARTERS IN
TRUNKS
—AND—
VALISES,
FROM THE CHEAPEST TO THE BEST.

Furniture.

L. A. SHIVE'S SONS,

Furniture Dealers,

207
West Market Street,
YORK, PA.

WE HAVE THE

Largest and best selected stock of Furniture in the City.

WE GUARANTEE PRICES TO BE SATISFACTORY.

☛ GIVE US A CALL.

PHOTOGRAPHERS,

20 S. George St., York, Pa.

To all those wishing Photographs taken in the latest style and finish, we would advise them to call and see the work of

SHADLE & BUSSER.

☞ ALL WORK GUARANTEED.

The Frysinger RAG CARPETS a Specialty.

SOLD AT THE

FRYSINGER
Carpet Store,

The Largest Carpet Store in York,

124 WEST MARKET STREET,

YORK, PA.

OBE. CULLISON, Proprietor.

BUY THE LATEST AND BEST

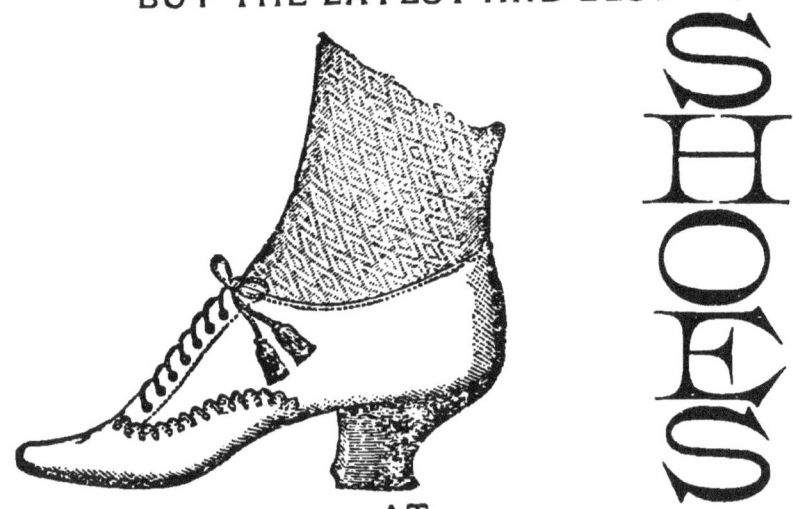

—AT—
Miller's Big Shoe Store,
YORK, PA.

☞ Gauze Oven Door
RANGE and STOVE.

Grand Times Cook,
    Altoona and Broadway Ranges,
Double Heater Ranges,
    Furnaces and Heating Stoves,
Plumbing, Tinners,
    Gas Work and Fixtures.

ALL KINDS REPAIRS.

HANTZ & JESSOP,
110 and 112 N. George St., YORK, PA.

☞ GAS, COOK AND HEAT STOVES. ☜

Weaver Organ AND Piano Co.

FACTORY AND WAREROOMS: BROAD AND WALNUT STS., } YORK, PA.

A PROPHET

Is not without honor save in his own country, but the

Weaver Organs

ARE MOST POPULAR WHERE THEY ARE BEST KNOWN.

Over 2,000 Sold in YORK COUNTY.

PIANOS AT WHOLESALE AND RETAIL.

IF YOU ARE IN NEED OF
DRUGS, MEDICINES,
TOILET ARTICLES,
SPONGES, BRUSHES,
SOAPS, &C., &C.

GO TO

SMALL'S
Leading Drug Store,

—21—

EAST MARKET STREET,

YORK, PA.

FACTORS OF

SMALL'S Liquid Rennet,

SMALL'S Flavoring Extracts,

SMALL'S Sarsaparilla,

SMALL'S Beef Wine and Iron,

SMALL'S Toothache Drops,

SMALL'S

Everything and anything you may need which is usually kept in a

First-Class Drug Store.

AT
D. W. CRIDER & BRO.,
Booksellers,
27 West Market Street,
YORK, PA.,

You will always find a well-selected stock of

BOOKS, SUNDAY SCHOOL REWARD CARDS, TEACHERS' BIBLES, FOUNTAIN GOLD PENS,

AND

A GENERAL LINE OF FINE STATIONERY, ALL THE LATEST SONG BOOKS.

AS THE AGENTS OF THE

United Brethren Publishing House of Dayton, Ohio,

All publications of the same can be secured of them.

ALL SUPPLIES NECESSARY FOR THE
Public Schools
KEPT IN STOCK.

www.ingramcontent.com/pod-product-compliance
Lightning Source LLC
Chambersburg PA
CBHW031120160426
43192CB00008B/1060